CHANGE AND GROW

TADPOLE TO FROG

Acknowledgements: Cover: getty images/Geoff Brightling, getty images/Joel Sartore, gettyimages/Dorling Kindersley, gettyimages/ Gail Shumway, gettyimages/American Images Inc. p1 gettyimages/Don Farrall, p2 gettyimages/Kim Taylor and Jane Burton, p3 gettyimages/Geoff Dann, pp4–5 gettyimages/Christoph Burki, p5 gettyimages/Altrendo Nature, p6 gettyimages/F Millington, p7 gettyimages/Neil Fletcher, gettyimages/Geoff Dann, gettyimages/Kim Taylor and Jane Burton, p8 gettyimages/Rosemary Calvert, p9 gettyimages/Kim Taylor and Jane Burton, p10 gattyimages/Kim Taylor and Jane Burton, p11 gettyimages/Dorling Kindersley, pp12–13 gettyimages/David J Green. p14 gettyimages/Dorling Kindersley, p15 gettyimages/Jason Edwards, p16 gettyimages/ Dorling Kindersley, p17 gettyimages/Dorling Kindersley, p18 gettyimages/Geoff Dann, pp18–19 gettyimages/Michael Redmer, p20 gettyimages/Jason Edwards, p21 gettyimages/Frank Greenaway, pp22–23 gettyimages/Cary Anderson, p23 gettyimages/Gerry Ellis, p24 gettyimages/ Geoff Dann.

First published by Parragon in 2009

Parragon
Queen Street House
4 Queen Street
Bath BA1 1HE, UK

ISBN 978-1-4075-8046-3

Printed in China

CHANGE AND GROW

TADPOLE TO FROG

Steve Parker

Bath · New York · Singapore · Hong Kong · Cologne · Delhi · Melbourne

Spring is Here!

Frogs spend the cold winter in a deep sleep called hibernation. As spring arrives, they wake up and get ready to breed.

A safe place to sleep

Frogs hibernate in damp, safe places away from the worst of the cold. They may bury themselves in mud or hide in a ditch or under roots or stones.

Time to wake up

The warm spring sunshine wakes the frogs up. They hop to the nearest pond to get together with other frogs.

Croak!

Getting together

The male croaks to attract a female. When he has found a mate, the male frog sits on her back. She is then ready to lay her eggs.

Frog Eggs

The female frog lays a lot of small, jellylike eggs in shallow water. The eggs clump together in a sticky mass called frog spawn.

Single cell

A frog starts life as a tiny black dot, called a cell, surrounded by jelly. The jelly provides food for the growing frog and protects it from the outside world.

Embryo

The black dot grows bigger and changes shape. It is now called an embryo. It has a head and a tail.

Ready to hatch

After about ten days, the embryo starts to eat its way through the jelly. Then it hatches.

7

I'VE ARRIVED!

**The newly hatched frog is called a tadpole.
It does not look at all like an adult frog.**

Sticking together
The tadpole sticks to its egg
using suckers on its head.
It stays like this for about
a week, feeding off the
remains of the food
stored inside the egg.

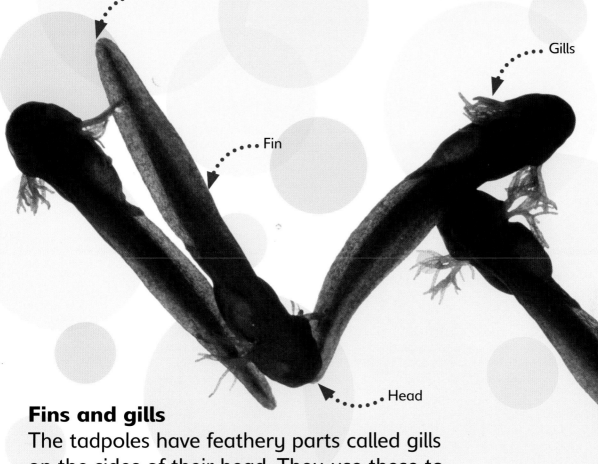

Tail

Gills

Fin

Head

Fins and gills

The tadpoles have feathery parts called gills on the sides of their head. They use these to breathe underwater. Their long tail has fins along the top and bottom to help with swimming.

TIME TO EAT

About ten days after hatching, the tadpole starts to swim around and look for food. It begins to grow very quickly.

Plant food
The young tadpole mainly eats plants. It scrapes up pond weeds and the green slime from pebbles.

Tadpoles have tough lips.

Staying together

At first the tadpoles stay in a group. If danger comes near, such as a hungry fish, they wriggle their tails and swim into waterweeds for safety.

GROWING FAST

As the tadpole grows, its head gets larger and rounder. It can swim faster. This is handy, because it has a lot of enemies, including newts, diving beetles, and waterbirds.

New gills
The tadpole loses its
feathery gills. It grows new gills
under flaps on the sides of its head.
The tadpole breathes water in through its mouth,
over the gills, and out through a hole called the spiracle.

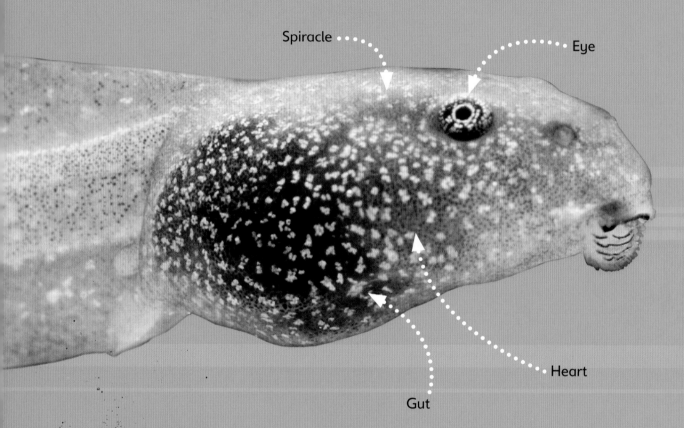

Spiracle

Eye

Heart

Gut

Curly guts
The tadpole's gut, or intestine, and its red heart show through its thin skin. The gut is where the tadpole takes in nourishment from food.

MOVING ON TO MEAT

After a few weeks of eating plants, the tadpole changes its tastes. It now starts to look for meaty food.

Finding food

The hungry tadpole goes after very small pond animals, such as water fleas, young pond snails, baby fish, and tiny worms.

Tadpoles eat tiny pieces of meat.

Hungry hunter

It will also munch on larger pieces of meat— even dead animals that fall into the water.

Head start

Next, the tadpole starts to
change shape. Its head starts to
look more like a frog's, with a
wide mouth for grabbing prey.

Time for a Change

About two months after hatching, really big changes begin to happen in the tadpole's body. Two back legs pop out—and then two front legs.

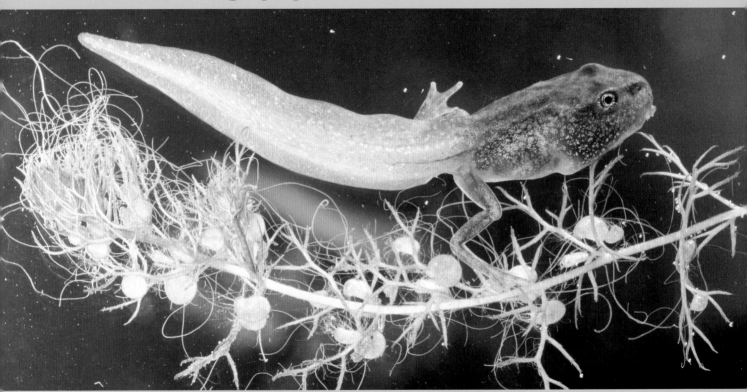

Back legs
The back legs push through the tadpole's skin. Each has five webbed toes.

Kicking out
The tadpole uses its kicking legs, as well as its wiggly tail, to swim.

Front legs

A week or two later, the front legs, or arms, push out through the tadpole's skin.

Reaching out

Each tiny hand has four fingers. The tadpole uses them to grasp water plants.

Skin is stretched between the fingers.

LOOK, NO TAIL!

After three or four months, the tadpole has changed into a baby frog, or froglet. It has four legs, a wide mouth, large eyes—and its tail is almost gone.

No need for a tail
The froglet can now jump as well as swim. Its tail starts to shrink, and it goes onto dry land for the first time.

A tadpole sees as well as an adult frog.

Metamorphosis

When a tadpole changes into a frog, it is called metamorphosis. Toads, newts, and salamanders also change in this way. All these animals are known as amphibians.

FROGLET AT LAST

**The froglet is now four or five months old.
It looks like a grown-up frog—but much smaller.
It's the size of the tip of your finger.**

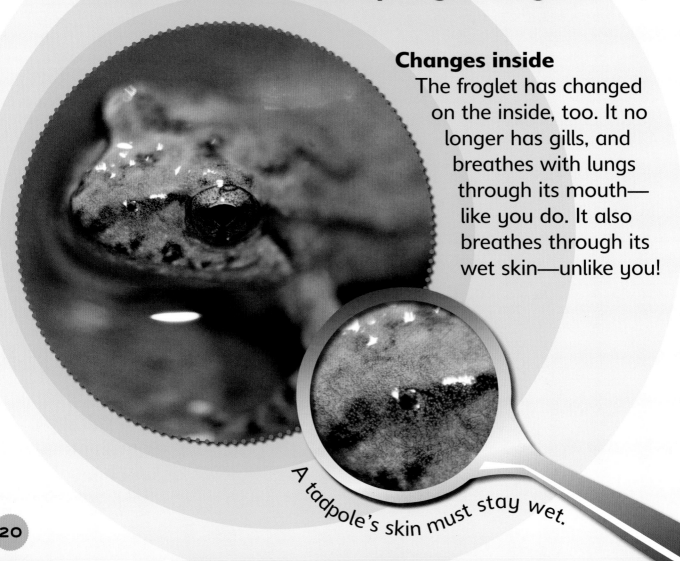

Changes inside

The froglet has changed on the inside, too. It no longer has gills, and breathes with lungs through its mouth—like you do. It also breathes through its wet skin—unlike you!

A tadpole's skin must stay wet.

I can see you!
The froglet feeds on small insects like gnats and midges. Just like an adult frog, it can see them above the water with its bulging eyes.

LEAVING THE POND

Fall arrives, the weather turns colder, and the froglet leaves the pond. It hops away to find a safe place for its first winter sleep.

Fall feast

Before hibernation, the froglet eats as much food as it can—worms, slugs, flies, and spiders are all on the menu.

Away from water

The froglet stays in damp, shady places, like long grass, for the next few years. It does not go back to the pond until it is full grown and ready to breed— three or four years later.

23

LIFE CYCLE

Mating
In spring, frogs gather together in ponds—the males croak to attract female mates.

Laying
The male and female mate and the female lays her eggs—known as frog spawn.

Full grown
Four years later the frog is full grown and ready to breed.

1–2 weeks
The tadpole hatches from its egg.

Life on land
The froglet stays on land for the next few years.

3–4 weeks
The tadpole starts to eat plant food. It breathes through outer gills.

First winter
In fall the froglet leaves the pond to spend its first winter on land.

5–6 weeks
The tadpole starts to eat meat. It grows inner gills.

13–16 weeks
The tadpole is now a froglet. It starts to hunt for tiny prey.

7–8 weeks
The tadpole's back legs appear.

11–12 weeks
The tail shrinks and the tadpole starts to breathe with lungs.

9–10 weeks
The tadpole's front legs appear.